We Served At Sea

HMS Ganges, boys' training establishment

We Served At Sea

David Sharp

TRUE
BOOKS

ISBN 978-0-9557472-0-5

Printed and bound in Great Britain by
Biddles Limited, King's Lynn, Norfolk

First published in the UK in 2007 by

True Books Limited
4 Cornwall House, Bird Wood Avenue, Deal, Kent CT14 9RY

For Sarah and John
who inspired me to write this book,
and gave me the encouragement to proceed.
Very many thanks.

GANGES

WISDOM IS STRENGTH

Acknowledgements

I would like to dedicate this book to the thousands of boys who passed through the portals of HMS GANGES and went on to serve with The Fleet, many of them with distinction – once a Ganges boy, always a Ganges boy.

I would like to thank all those who assisted me with their kind co-operation during the research for this book, far too many to mention. I am sure they will forgive me for not being able to list them all. I would like to thank in particular The HMS Ganges Association, The Ganges Museum, and The Royal Naval Association.

Contents

Chapter One

The Beginning

After the war, HMS GANGES was re-established as a boys' training establishment, with its primary training objective to turn out disciplined, responsible, and self-reliant young men, possessing confidence, courage, endurance, and a sense of service, professionally trained to take their place in the fleet.

And so it was, as I neared the main gates, that a feeling of nostalgia overcame me. These events happened to me over fifty years ago. As I stood looking through the gates, the security guard came strolling over to me.

'You another Ganges boy, then?' he enquired.

'I just thought I would take a last look round the place,' I replied.

'Would you like to have a wander around?'

'I would like to very much.'

He undid the gates for me and let me inside.

'Take as long as you like, mate; give me a call when you've finished.'

The mast was still there. It was a landmark; you could see it for miles around. As I slowly walked across the parade ground, now sadly covered with weeds, in my memory I could hear the drill instructors calling out the commands: 'By the right dress, quick march, slope arms,' etc. Most of the buildings I remembered had been knocked down but the signal tower was still standing. We were trained to read Morse code sent by flashing lights. I spent about an hour walking around, re-living all those memories.

Back at the main gates, I called the security guard.

'Did you see all you wanted?' he asked.

'Yes thanks,' I replied, 'not much of the old place left now. I'm sorry to see its going to be turned into a housing development.'

'Aye,' he said, 'I suppose that's what you call progress.'

With that he returned to his hut, no doubt back to his cup of tea and his newspaper.

As I sat in my car, it all came flooding back to me. The year was 1948, a cold February morning just two months into the New Year. I stood on the mainline platform at Victoria Station in Nottingham with my mother, who had come to see me off. The train would take me to my new career with the Royal Navy. I had been accepted as a boy entrant to be trained at HMS GANGES, where I would serve out my two years Boy service. At last the train came slowly puffing into the platform. I gave my mother a hug and promised to write as soon as they would let me. I noticed a group of four boys further down the platform, clutching their suitcases, just like me. We got together, and yes, we were all going to the same place. As we got chatting, we learned we were all from different backgrounds and walks of life, but we all had one thing in common: we wanted to join the Navy. Next stop – London, then on to Ipswich. I had never been this far from home and all its comforts.

I shall never forget our arrival at Ipswich station. Standing by the ticket barrier was, as I was to learn later, a Petty Officer instructor.

'OK, Ganges lads, this way.' It was a cold winter's night and raining as usual. 'Follow me,' he said. We were led outside and saw two Naval lorries parked in the car park. 'Right lads, up you get into the lorries.'

They had a large RN painted on their sides. It was nice to get in out of the rain. Two of the lads in the back of the lorry lit up cigarettes, much to the annoyance of the Petty Officer. 'Put those fags out; I'll tell you when you can smoke,' he shouted. 'Look, the lot of you,' he said in a not unkindly voice, 'I'll tell you when you can smoke – you're in the Navy now. When you arrive at Ganges, one of the first things you will learn is discipline. Forget everything you have learnt; there are three ways of doing things in the Navy – the book way, the navy way, and my way. If you remember these three rules, you won't go far wrong. You can't buck the system.'

It seemed an age sitting in the lorry, but at long last we had arrived. 'Get your kit and fall in two ranks.' We found ourselves standing among a group of Nissan huts, painted green, with white painted stones along all the paths. 'Pay attention now,' said the Petty Officer. 'This is your new home for the next eight weeks. It's called the Annexe, and is where you will complete your basic training. When I call out your names, fall in by the hut. We call them messes.

My name was called, along with twelve others, and we entered the mess. On each side of the mess were single iron beds, piled high with sheets and blankets, and between each bed were steel cupboards.

'We call them lockers,' said Yeo Minter. 'You've got just ten minutes to make up your beds and then fall in outside. We will march over to the dining hall for supper.'

The main gate to HMS Ganges

And with that, the P.O. disappeared. I soon made up my bed, but the lad next to me was having trouble. 'Sod this for a lark! Me mum makes my bed at home.' He had a broad Geordie accent you could cut with a knife.

'Come on mate, I'll help you,' I said to him.

'Coo, thanks mate. I just hope the scran is good here, I'm starving. I ate all the grub me mum and sister made for me.'

P.O. Minter arrived back in the mess. 'Right you lot, fall in outside and we will march to supper. Cut the cackle and cut out sky-larking. When you've had your supper, you can have thirty minutes in the canteen. I want you back in the mess by 2030; that's 8.30 to you, Geordie. Lights out at 2200 hours; you've all got a very full day tomorrow.

The supper – sausage, egg, and chips – washed down by hot, sweet tea, as much as you wanted, was very good. 'This is more like it!' said Geordie, 'Can we have seconds?' After we had eaten, we drifted back to the mess. I for one was ready for bed; it had been a long day. As I drifted off to sleep, I thought my dream of joining the navy had come true.

Yeo Minter came back into the mess. 'Get a good night's sleep, lads, you will have a busy day tomorrow. Wakey, wakey will be at 0530.' With that he turned out the lights; I was happy, and wondered what the next few weeks would bring.

'Wakey, wakey! Rise and shine. The sun is scorching your eyes out.' (Can't be. It's February.) It was Yeo Minter. 'You have exactly thirty minutes to make your beds, wash and shave.' (Well, wash anyway).

'Hells bloody bells!' said Geordie in the next bed. 'It's the middle of the bloody night. I'm not getting up yet!' He pulled the sheets back over his head.

Suddenly there was a terrific crash. Poor Geordie's bed was on top of him, and he lay in a tangle of sheets, blankets, and bedstead. 'Out now or I'll know the reason why,' said Yeo Minter.

'Yes Yeo, yes Yeo', Geordie said in a very shaky voice, and was then seen running to the showers as fast as he could.

Class of 1949/50 Hawke Division
Author is shown ringed in the back row.

Yeo Minter was smothering a smile; 'I told him, The navy or my way. OK lads, this is our programme for today: 0900 kit issue, this will take us until lunch time. As none of you draw your tots yet, you can go to the canteen for half an hour. This reminds me when I was on the old Swiftsure...' and he would go off with one of his stories. He kept us all spellbound. 'Right, back to realities, I want you all back in the mess by 1330 hours to lay out your kit. It should take you the rest of the day.'

As I was issued with my kit, I thought, 'This is the first time in my life I have ever had any new clothes.' My mother found it hard to bring up two boys on her small wages, as we had no father to support us. Whilst serving in the R.A.F. as a rear gunner during the war, he had been shot down and killed over Germany. Back in the mess, Yeo Minter showed us how to lay out our kit.

'You will all have been issued with a wooden stencil showing your names,' he said, 'mark all your kit with it, and I do mean everything! I'll show you how to do a chain stitch later on. Now pay attention', he said. 'Rig of the day – blue uniform shirt (no. 8s). Working dress – blue trousers, boots and gaiters, not forgetting your cap. You will salute all Officers – you can't mistake them – they have gold bands on their arms – but not Petty Officers or Chief Petty Officers. Got that? Good! If in any doubt, ask me; that's what I'm here for.'

The day seemed to fly by. All too soon it was time to turn in with only one last job to do. We had all been given a postcard to enable us to write to our parents to let them know we had arrived safely. The following weeks seemed to pass very quickly. We learned to march, tell left from right – some of the lads found it a little difficult – Geordie for one!

We were now doing things as a team, or the navy way. Even Geordie began to settle down, much to the delight of Yeo Minter.

Passing out parade at HMS Ganges

Today – the day of all days – Passing out parade. We had done our eight weeks of basic training and were leaving the Annexe – Nozzers no more. We were to go to the HMS GANGES main establishment at Shotley. As we marched smartly on to the parade ground, with the band of The Royal Marines leading the way, I would not have swapped my place for anything in the world. I knew this was where I belonged.

We had achieved so much in so short a time. We all felt very proud of ourselves; I for one couldn't wait to get to sea, but that would be a long way in the future.

Chapter Two

Training

Today we begin our sixteen months' training in earnest. It will involve signalling by light, flags, and Morse code. We are told the pass mark will be 22 words a minute. We have boat work to look forward to, and all the sport we can play. We will have to master also the 303 Lee Enfield rifle, to shoot it and march with it. I only had one daunting thought – I can't swim yet – but no doubt the navy will soon teach me how.

Early one March morning, we were marched to the mast by Yeo Minter. Looking up, it seemed to tower above us. 'Look, you lads', he said. 'All boys have to climb it, four at a time.' I was in the first group. 'I want you to climb to the top, and not through the Lubbers Hole.'

'Blimey,' said Geordie, 'not with boots and gaiters on, Yeo?'

'You climb as you are. First four, away you go.'

I'm sure we all had butterflies in our stomachs. The Yeo told us it was 156 feet high and swayed in the wind. Taking a deep breath, I began to climb. Conquering my fear, I began to go up. The rope rungs were covered in frost and ice. At last I had reached the main yardarm; I had to climb outwards and upwards. I reached up and hauled through to stand on the island – I was half way up. Only another 80 feet to go. At long last I reached the top. What a view! You could see for miles in any direction. I began to wonder why I had such a sleepless night last night, worrying about the mast climb. Now all I had to do was to climb down.

Looking back on these activities, I can see the logic of the exercises. It is to make you have faith in yourself; if you could do this, you could do anything.

As I write this story, certain events seem to stick in the mind. I shall always remember one such event. It was a Saturday morning. I had been selected to play cricket for the Division and was happily batting away in the nets when I was told to report to the swimming baths. On my arrival, I could see about another twenty boys standing in the lobby.

'You wanted me, sir?'

'Yes, you're a non-swimmer, Sharp. Fall in with the rest of the group.'

He was the senior PTI (Physical Training Instructor). 'You have all got five minutes to get changed into swimming trunks and report back here.' The swimming pool was of Olympic standard, with the top diving board sixty feet above the water. 'What I want you to do is climb to the top board and jump in. You will see around the sides of the pool other instructors holding poles. When you come up, grab a pole and you will be pulled into the side. Got that?' the PTI asked. 'OK, away you go. Just one thing to remember: if you can't swim, you will not get a ship!'

The author saluting at the top of the mast

Having heard this frightening news, I climbed up to the top board, took a deep breath and jumped. It seemed an age before I came spluttering to the surface. I saw a pole and grabbed it and was pulled into the side. 'Well done lad, now do it again and again.'

After five exhausting weeks, I managed to swim one length of the pool, dressed in a duck suit (canvas top and trousers). I managed to stay afloat for the required three minutes and passed my swimming test. At least now I'll get a ship, I thought.

Another event was Christmas leave – two whole beautiful weeks to do what you like, go where you like, have a beer, swagger down the street in your bell-bottom trousers. Jolly Jack Tar with all the girls wanting to touch your collar for luck. It seemed very strange, nobody shouting at you, telling you what to do.

However, after about five days I began to get bored and wanted to return to the life I had come to know, the life in the navy; back to the boats, signalling, and to the comradeship of my mess mates. In any case, I was looking forward to the forthcoming regatta. I was coxswain of the whaler 14 Alpha with four of my pals as crew. We stood a good chance of winning another silver trophy for the divisional collection.

Looking back on those sixteen months, I had my sixteenth and seventeenth birthdays at Ganges; we were taught a lot – seamanship, signalling, and to read Morse code and light at 22 words a minute, and a whole lot more. I would not have missed this training for anything in the world. All the friends I had made; we would see each other from time to time within the service. In the navy you made friends for life.

Our class as a whole passed out on 10th March 1950 and we went our separate ways. Our group, together with Yeo Minter, was drafted to the Carrier HMS Neptune. We were to join her as signal boys 2nd class. At last I was in the real Royal Navy.

Our last evening at HMS Ganges, sitting with our two instructors and their wives, before we set sail for Korea

That same day, our sailing orders came through; we were ordered to Korea. The Neptune carries a crew of 1,320 officers and ratings, 24 Sea Vixen aircraft, and 4 helicopters; in addition, a complement of 120 Royal Commandos. We were a force to be reckoned with. We joined the ship at Portsmouth. There was to be no shore leave. We were to sail the following morning at 0630 hours. As always with the Navy, you sail at the crack of dawn.

Chapter Three

The Landing

Life on board a carrier is a very ordered affair. The ship is so vast it is like living in a small town, with all departments interlocked. Our B boys' mess was three decks down, and in fact we were below the water line. To get to the signals Bridge we had to climb up eight decks. It took some getting used to. When we eventually got there, we tried to make ourselves small. We were very much the new boys. However, the Chief Yeoman teamed us up with some of the more experienced ratings, so that we could learn the ropes. It felt good to be standing on the signal deck as we left the harbour. We looked a brave sight, flags streaming in the wind, all the hands fallen in for leaving harbour. There were only a few people to see us off; just a few navy wives and their children to wave a last goodbye.

As we cleared the harbour approaches, our destroyer escort was ordered to form line astern; they fell in behind us. The Captain turned to the commander. 'We shall exercise action stations in half an hour.' We were on a war footing. 'Hoist Zebra Jig intro One Steer 185 degrees, speed 16 knots; standby with flag fox.' Our signal to receive our aircraft. These had been based ashore. I remembered the next two hours – it was a blur of noise of alarm bells ringing and of our aircraft landing on the carrier – but it was very orderly. As soon as an aircraft landed on the deck it was manhandled to the lifts and was taken to the hangar deck to be re-fuelled and re-armed. We were told that the Chinese army had crossed the 39th parallel.

Carrier HMS Neptune

We had been on board now for five weeks and getting to know the ship's routine well. Apart from a brief stop at Gibraltar to re-fuel and to top up our supplies, but no shore leave, our next stop was the island of Gan in the Indian Ocean. Our aircraft were in the air from morning to night, exercising bombing and strafing runs in all kinds of weather.

As we progressed further into the Indian Ocean, we left the dull weather far behind us. The days were long, with bright sunshine. I was getting a nice tan from being on the flag deck for most of the day, but we were all soon to learn that this was not a pleasure cruise, and we were told our part in the forthcoming operations.

The Chief Yeoman told us to report to the plot room next morning at 0800 hours to be briefed. Next morning on the dot, we signalmen were gathered in the plot room; the air was thick with tobacco smoke. Overnight, the wind had got up to force 8; we could feel the ship's motion as she rolled first to port, then with a sickening motion, she rolled to starboard with a corkscrew motion. Some of the lads were beginning to feel seasick. The Chief Yeoman entered the plot room. 'Good God! It's thick in here. Open the scuttles and let some air in,' he said. 'Settle down, the Commander Air will be here soon to tell you about our part in this operation. Listen to what he has to say; make notes if you want to.'

Commander Air stepped into the plot room. I had only seen him from a distance before, but I had heard of his exploits as a pilot, and was very impressed. His pilots would follow him anywhere. How's that for leadership? He was forty years old but looked about thirty. He stood over six feet tall, three gold rings on his arm, with the pilots wings above. To get this far in his career, he had done well.

'Good morning, lads; smoke if you want to.' The Chief Yeoman looked up at the deck head and shrugged his shoulders. 'I'll try to put you in the picture. We will be up against some of the worst terrorist troops you can imagine.

Our job will be to punch a hole through their lines to allow our own troops to land and obtain a secure foothold. You signalmen will be landed to act as spotting teams. I'll tell you what's required of you once you are ashore and have established radio contact with the ship.' We noticed that behind the commander, covered over with a dustsheet, was a map of the southern-most tip of Korea. 'Gather round so you can all see.' The map was divided into sections. 'These are grid references of the local area. Our aircraft will already be airborne and can be over the target area in minutes, either to carry out a bombing mission or a strafing run. All I can say is, remember your training, speak slowly. We on the ship will be relying on you and your teams. Good luck and do the best you can. I'll now hand over to the signals officer.' As he left the plot room he was heard to say, 'Good luck: they are going to need it.'

Lt Cdr Harris, our signals Officer and mentor, came into the plot room. 'I'll now tell you the codes and signalling procedure for this operation. You will carry ship to shore radios and signal flags. You will all be armed with rifles; each group will carry a sten gun. The two Yeomen will also carry pistols and, in addition, each of you will carry six grenades. You'll have rations for twenty-four hours. Are there any questions? No? Good! Report to the armoury at 1630 to be issued with your weapons.'

As the officers left the plot room, we all sat in silence, wondering what tomorrow would bring. 'Well Dave, what do you make of that?' Yeo Minter asked. Like everyone else I felt a little apprehensive. Could I stand up to what the morrow would bring?

The author

'It's the same old story, Yeo,' I said. 'If you can't take a joke, you shouldn't have joined.'

'Gather round,' said the Chief Yeoman. 'If any of you have any letters to write, I think now would be a good time.'

I wrote a quick note to my mother; she knew where we were through the newspaper reports. 'I'm fine, everything OK; looking forward to next leave. Don't worry, I have some nice presents for you. See you soon.'

Freddy Fox, my pal on and off the rugby field said, 'It'll be OK, Dave. I'm just a little bit scared.'

'Sure it will, Freddy. We will all be together, us against the rest. After this we should get some leave and you can see that lovely girl of yours. Come on mate, let's go and get some supper,' I said. When we got back to the mess, there was no good-natured bantering or skylarking; this was it, as serious as it can get. We all wondered what the next 48 hours would bring, away from the security of the ship and our messmates.

Tuesday 0330 hours – I felt someone shaking my hammock. 'Come on Dave, time to get up.' It was Nobby Hill, the Quartermaster. 'I've made a brew, it's hot and sweet,' he said. 'The Captain wants to see all the landing party in the hangar deck at 0430 hours. Breakfast is ready for you in the dining hall.' None of us felt much like eating this morning.

One hour later, we were mustered on the hangar deck, festooned with our weapons and equipment. The landing craft stood ready to be winched over the side to take us ashore. The Captain came down the steps from the bridge.

'Chief Yeoman, gather your party round.' The skipper had been on the bridge for the past 36 hours without a break but had made the time to see us off. His responsibility was enormous. He told us that the weather was not improving, with fog and snow flurries; also that the temperature was dropping.

'We are four miles off shore; this is as close as I can get. It will be a rough ride, but for your own protection you will be landing in the dark. I know that you can do it; it's what you have been trained for. I wish you all god speed and good luck. We will be relying on you.'

The landing craft was lowered over the ship's side with us aboard. 'Let go', yelled the coxswain and we hit the water. We began to roll heavily from side to side, with spray breaking over the blunt bows; soon we were all soaked to the skin, trying to keep our equipment dry, especially the radio. Some of the lads quickly succumbed to the unsteady motion of the vessel and were seasick in the scuppers.

It remained icy cold. We could only see a few feet ahead because of this fog. All our nerves were stretched taut, not knowing what was ahead. Apart from the two Yeomen, our average age was 17 years.

At long last our nightmare journey was nearly over; we could just make out the shore line ahead. Above the noise of the surf and the engine, the coxswain shouted, 'Lock and load, we are nearly in.' With a tremendous crash, the ramp came down – we were right on the beach. We all waded ashore.

Gathering our equipment, we grouped together on the

beach. The Chief Yeoman and his party moved off to the left. We all shook hands and wished each other good luck. It was the last we were to see of them. We were all feeling the cold, but sweat was running down my back. 'Dave,' said Freddy, 'how far have we to go?'

'About four miles, looking at the map. Just keep going, we'll make it OK,' I told him. What a place! The landscape was desolate, with rocky outcrops scattered around, which made the going very hard, loaded with our equipment.

Yeo Minter took a bearing with the compass. 'We're on the right track; we can't be far off now,' he said.

We were looking for hill 64 according to the map reference, which was to be our spotting post. Pete Riller took the lead. In the distance we could hear the occasional burst of gunfire and explosions. It was still snowing and very misty. A deep chill was in the air; we couldn't see for more than a few yards in front of us.

Soon it was broad daylight and we could see where we were going. It seemed like we had been walking for hours; we pressed on.

'After all,' said Freddy, 'we are sailors, not bloody pongees. I'll be glad to get there and rest a while.'

At last we could see hill 77 baker, our home for the next few hours. We were spot on. The hill was about 450 feet high, giving a good view of the plain in front of us. At the very top was a rocky ledge, with a sort of basin running around the rim. This is where we set up our post.

Our party had been on this godforsaken rock for four hours. We were all cold and hungry. There was an eerie silence about the place. We spread ourselves around the rock rim, keeping our heads down. We tried to peer into the fog, which seemed like a curtain. As the daylight came creeping in, a weak sunshine made the landscape in front of us look like a fairy tale picture we remembered from childhood. As the mist lifted, we could see for about five miles in any direction from our vantage point above.

Big Tony, the Londoner, who was shivering and, like the rest of us, trying to keep warm said, 'Dave, ask the Yeo if we can have a fag, I'm gasping.'

'Yes, I can hear you; light up if you must. I'll have one too, but remember to keep them covered up. The glow can be seen from a long distance and can give our position away,' the Yeo replied.

'Dave,' shouted Freddy, who was on lookout, 'can you see this?' I took his binoculars and looked over the edge of the rim. In the distance we could see orange gun flashes and, coming towards our positions, troops advancing on us.

'Bloody hell! They must know we are somewhere here,' Yeo called. 'I make it about two miles away. Get on the radio and give map references and ask for a bombing run and strafing run a.s.a.p.'

The snow began to fall again as if we didn't have enough troubles. All of us, to tell the truth, were scared. We had heard what the Communist troops did to their prisoners if we were captured. I got through to the ship and gave them co-ordinates. Where the hell were our aircraft? I was bitterly cold but could feel the sweat running down my back. We checked our weapons once again. It was not unknown for them to freeze up in these temperatures and we wanted to make sure they would fire.

'I can't stand much more of this,' Freddy said, trying to bury his body into the rocks.

Half an hour must have passed. The mist appeared to have lifted a little. The oncoming troops seemed to have stopped. We made a brew to help us fight off the cold. Chalky, who was on lookout, remarked, 'It's bloody quiet.' He spoke too soon.

Every hill around our position was subjected to an intense bombardment of artillery fire. There were explosions all around us. All the surrounding area was covered with smoke and flame. The next thing I remember, I was lying on the ground with an agonising pain in my back. I must have blacked out.

When I came to, and my hearing slowly returned, I could hear the sound of gunfire getting closer. I put my hand to the small of my back; it came away thick with blood. I had never felt such pain. I could see the Yeo lying over the rim of the crater; the back of his head had been blown off. There was nothing I could do for him. Chalky lay slumped over the radio. I could see he was dead too. We must have taken a direct hit. I pulled myself to the rim's edge but the mist had come down again; I could see nothing.

It was beginning to get dark now and we could still hear gunfire in the distance. Then I could just make out behind me a low moaning noise. It seemed to be behind the rocks. I crawled over. Freddy lay crumpled up.

'Is that you, Dave? I can't feel my legs.'

'Let me check you over, mate.' I was feeling very groggy myself; my trousers were wet with blood. I looked down to Freddy's legs – my God – his left foot had been blown off above the ankle. He was losing a lot of blood. I took off his belt and made him a tourniquet, making it as tight as I could. All I could do, apart from bandaging his stump, was to give him a shot of morphine. He was passing in and out of consciousness and calling for his mother. 'Look Freddy, we shall have to move out of here. The sods have us zeroed in.' We began the painful journey to our new position about 400 yards up hill. At last we made it. I blacked out again.

When I came to again, it all seemed a blur. I must have been weak from the loss of blood from my wound. Freddy was still out cold. I felt isolated and alone, but I was getting angry. I hauled myself up to the rim of our hideaway. 'Come on, you bastards. You've killed my best friends but I'll take some of you with me,' I shouted as I angled the sten at the approaching troops. 'Freddy', I said, 'I must go back for the radio.'

I managed to crawl to our old position, and grabbed the radio. I tested it. Thank God, it was still working. It was a good job that I had decided to move our position because at that moment a mortar round landed and exploded in the exact spot we were in a few moments ago. I must have blacked out again, for when I came to it was quite dark and still snowing. Freddy was still crying out for his mother. All I could do was to give him another shot of morphine to ease his pain.

The enemy troops were still advancing towards us. I hope the radio still works! 'Tango one, tango one, how do you read? Over.'

'Plot one, loud and clear.' How nice to hear a friendly voice.

'Situation report as follows: five dead, two wounded; do you read me? Over. Request instructions; over.' I replaced the mike. I could hear a sound, like baying wolves.

Looking over the edge, I could see it was the enemy coming towards us. They were no more than 800 yards away. I got back on to the radio and called the ship again, giving them map references. Right on top of us; this is it now; is this what it's like to die? I got the sten ready. Single shots only. I began firing and threw three hand grenades over for good measure. The air around me was suddenly torn apart by machine gun fire. Our aircraft were coming in at no more than 200 feet, bombing and strafing the oncoming troops. I must have blacked out again; I don't remember anything after that.

When I came to again, it was to see the grave face of our ship's surgeon bending over me. As my eyes began to focus again, everything seemed blurred and unreal.

'You have had quite a time of it, lad,' he said to me. 'I removed some pieces of shrapnel from your back. As soon as arrangements can be made, we shall fly you back home to the Royal Naval Hospital, Haslar, at Portsmouth, where you can be treated. Now don't worry, the Marines found you when they landed.'

'Sir,' I asked, trying to sit up in bed. 'Signalman Fox, how is he?'

'We found him just in time. We have operated on his foot, and in time he will recover. He will be fitted with an artificial foot. He won't play rugby any more, poor Freddy;

he loved the game; but at least he's alive. Now lay back, the Captain wants to have a quick word.'

'Yes sir.' I was a bit overawed.

'I have just come to say how very proud of you we all are. Thanks to your actions we have managed to make the breakthrough. I am recommending you for a decoration. Now get some rest.'

The surgeon commander was bending over me again. 'I'm just going to give you a small injection to help you sleep.'

I felt a gentle prick in my arm and remembered no more.

Chapter Four

Interlude

It was now three months since I had left the Carrier. Here I was in the ordered world of the hospital, under the watchful eye of Sister June Allison. I guess all the patients were a little in love with her. She put on a stern 'no nonsense' attitude, but when recovering from an operation she was kindness itself. Gradually, as the days passed, I was beginning to feel my old self once again. I was feeling well and wanted to be up and about again. They let me walk around the gardens holding on to the nurse's arm. A red letter day today – I have a visitor – Freddy Fox and his mother. He was being fitted with his artificial foot, but sadly, he was to be discharged from the Navy. Words were said about our time on the rock – enough said. We wished each other well and said our goodbyes. He now lives in Australia and is running his own business, together with his wife.

Friday, 10th May – my all important interview with the senior surgeon to see if they would pass me fit for duty again. The interview was attended by another two doctors. I began to feel my stomach turn over. 'Good morning Sharp. Please take a seat. You have been with us for nearly five months and have made a good recovery. I am pleased to tell you I shall pass you fit for duty with the fleet, but first you will take three weeks' sick leave. Afterwards you will be appointed to another ship.' He shook my hand and that was that! I said goodbye to the nursing staff and thanked them for all the care they had shown me, collected my travel warrant and was off home.

On my arrival home, my mother hugged me. It was good to be home again. All the relations were there. They had laid on a 'welcome home' party for me. Now came the questions – Aunt Dorothy: 'Did you see any Chinese?'; Uncle Don: 'What was it like?' They all meant well, but all I wanted was to go to my own room and sleep. My leave was passing quickly and it would soon be time for me to report to HMS Victory, the Naval Barracks at Portsmouth, and to find out about my new ship.

Four days before my leave was to end, Mother called me, 'David, there's an official letter here for you.'

'I bet it's about my next ship,' I replied. It was a buff-coloured envelope with the Royal Crest on the front. Inside was a short note: 'You will report to the officer in charge at the investiture at Buckingham Palace at 1300 hours, Monday 8th June. You may bring a close relative with you.' I was to be presented with the D.S.C.; also inside the envelope was a travel warrant for two 1st class return tickets. My mother was very proud.

All too soon the leave was over. Secretly I was itching to get back to sea. The next morning I arrived at the barracks and reported to the regulating office.

'Name?' asked the junty (Naval policeman). He looked

in his file. 'Sharp, yes, I've got your draft chit here,' he said. 'You are to join HMS Salisbury. Tomorrow, transport will be laid on for you to take you to the Dockyard. Report back here at 0730 hours in the morning. In the meantime, go to the transit mess and settle in.' This mess was used for people who would not be staying more than 24 hours. The junty told me that the ship would be sailing for Singapore in the next couple of days.

Salisbury was a frigate with a crew of 200 officers and men; a displacement of 950 tonnes. She was armed with a 4-inch gun forward, two 2-pounders – anti aircraft guns, mounted aft in quadruple mountings. She had a speed of 16 knots. I was looking forward to serving in her. Next morning I reported to the office as instructed. The promised transport was waiting. I loaded my kit and we set off for the Dockyard. It was the second time I had been inside the Dockyard – everything was nestle and bustle. As we clattered over the train lines, the driver said, 'There she is.' She looked very smart with her white ensign flowing astern.

I unloaded my kit by the gangway. The officer of the Watch and the quartermaster were standing inboard. I saluted him and said in a rather shaky voice, 'Boy signalman Sharp come aboard to join, sir.'

'Welcome aboard, Sharp, we've been expecting you. Relax and get your kit on board; the quartermaster will show you your mess.'

For the next few days I was getting to know my way about the ship, and also met some of the crew. In charge of our signals department was Yeo Pole, a tall, cheerful

Scot. He had been in the navy for the past 20 years. Next in line was Leading Signalman Porter, who was in charge of our mess. It was a wonderful feeling of belonging. (Those of you who have been in the Service will understand.)

And so we sailed for Singapore. Our first stop was to be Gibraltar, with shore leave this time round on the Rock. It was strange to see British policemen and red phone boxes. All the streets were thronged with every kind of uniform you can imagine, and bustling throngs of people. All the shops were brightly lit and selling all kinds of merchandise. I bought my mother a pure silk scarf and a Japanese jewellery box. When opened it played a tune. I posted them off to her that same day. We were soon under sailing orders to proceed – Freetown, Simonstown, then across the vast emptiness of the Indian Ocean, on to Trickomele, and finally Singapore itself.

When I said our voyage was uneventful, life on passage was not. For example, 'Crossing the Line.' I had never done this before but you had to enter into the spirit of the thing. Our biggest and tallest seaman on board was Taffy Jones, an engine room rating, who always seemed to get into scrapes when ashore. He was always in the First Lt's Report. He would be King Neptune for the day. He was dressed in a mop cap with a grass skirt, a cardboard crown on his head, and carrying a trident, made for him by the engine room boys. He had two assistants dressed in the same way. In front of the 'Court' was a canvas chair which was overlooking a canvas pool into which they had made a mixture of foam from a local fire extinguisher, soft soap, and old engine oil from the engine room. We were made to sit in the canvas chair, facing backwards, and await results. My turn came – 'Who is this little runt who wishes to cross my kingdom?' yelled Taffy, now really enjoying himself.

I blurted out, laughingly, 'I am a small signalman with no importance. I wish to cross your kingdom, sir.'

The author, waiting for his bath

'You little sprog, you. I'll grant your wish, but first you will have to be shaved, that's if I can find any hairs on your chin; also you will need a bath. You little runts seem to smell.' With the help of his two assistants, I was shaved and bathed and ducked into the gunge. At last they let me up. I had crossed the Line. It was good fun for the first time.

Our other pastimes were tombola or bingo. The NAAFI shop opened at 1730 hours for the sale of the crew's beer ration, two cans per man. As I was still under age, it was Coke or a soft drink. If the weather was kind we would have a film show on the upper deck, followed by a singsong. Happy days!

For the next couple of weeks we all had to turn to to paint ship. In our case, the flag deck. We wanted to look smart when we entered Singapore harbour, under the keen scrutiny of the Base Commander. As we slowly approached the wide anchorage, we could see in the distance the reflected glare of the causeway which linked Singapore Island with the Mainland. The harbour itself was beset with stately sampans, scurrying water taxis, and some tall weathered junks with their latten sails. It was a constant hive of activity. As we approached our moorings, we could feel the heat of the sun now we were away from the sea breezes. All along the waterfront were tall gleaming white buildings. The streets were thronged with people, a mixture of Indian, Chinese and Malays. Rickshaws were criss-crossing the roads; there were food stalls all along each side of the streets. I had never seen anything like it before.

We berthed port side to and began to tidy up the flag deck. Sparks came clomping up the ladder to the Bridge. 'Signal, sir, for the Captain from S.N.O. Singapore (Senior Naval Officer). Captain report flagship at 1800 hours.'

'Acknowledge,' said the Captain. 'Finished with main engines.' With that he went below. We did the same.

The next day was Sunday, and in the tradition of the Service, the Captain held a church parade on the quarter-deck. We were all dressed in our best white uniforms. Our officers reported to the Captain that the divisions were ready for inspection. We had the Lord's Prayer, the Naval hymn, and the Naval prayer, 'Almighty God, who compasses the waters with lost bounds.' It always brings a lump to my throat. After Divisions we all looked to Sunday dinner, usually a roast; then make and mend, head down for a couple of hours, then look forward to our first run ashore in Singapore.

We had already had a talk by our ship's doctor about the perils of 'loose women' and the after-effects. Soon the welcome pipe of 'Up Spirits, stand fast the Holy Ghost'; the ship was soon filled with the heady smell of rum, then the pipe 'Hands to dinner' (Officers to lunch). This always raised a laugh. The next few hours were for ourselves. We had changed our money into dollars, and off we went to see the sights of Singapore (but that's another story!). Today was also my 18th birthday, and so I had my first tot of rum. At last, in the Navy's eyes I was classed as a man.

The next morning the Captain called all the ship's company to the quarterdeck and told us our programme for the next few months. We were to patrol the Malacca Straits, a waterway about 1,000 miles long and 80 miles wide. At the northern end was our sister ship HMS Pelew. Our brief was to stop and search any suspicious vessels; also to be on the lookout for ships smuggling arms or drugs. There was a lot of terrorist activity inland. The army patrols could only do so much; a big job in itself. However, before we started, the officers were to hold a party on the quarterdeck.

The Admiral enjoyed parties, but the main reason for holding one was to thank all the port staff for all the help and assistance they had given us since our arrival. The party was to be held on the following Saturday at 1900 hours. The ship's electrical staff would rig up a tannoy system attached to our music centre so that the guests would have dance music. The whole of the quarterdeck was to be covered with a taut white awning in case the weather turned. As bunting tossers, we were to drape signal flags down the sides to enclose the area. The officers' cooks were to provide the buffet-style food, and the wardroom Petty Officer and his three staff would set up a bar to serve drinks to the guests.

As the time for the party approached, we were sitting in the mess having a cup of coffee at stand easy. It was Friday morning. The First Lt came down to the mess. We had got to know him quite well, working on the flag deck as we did. He said, 'If any of you are not on duty or going ashore tomorrow night, we could use your help. The P.O. Steward has only three staff to assist. I would like three volunteers to help. It will only be a matter of taking trays of drinks and food round to the guests.' Three of us volunteered to help. 'Thank you. Please report to the P.O. Steward at 1830 hours, rig of the day will apply.'

As he turned to leave the mess he called me over. 'We have had a word with the Yeoman and your Divisional officer, Lt Hogarth. We have recommended that you sit for your Leading Signalmens exam shortly. I'll let you know the details at a later date.'

'Help,' I thought. If I manage to pass I would be one of the youngest Leading Signalmen in the Navy. Mum would be pleased with the extra money.

Saturday arrived, and we three reported to John, the P.O. Steward on the quarterdeck to ask about our duties. 'OK, P.O., what do you want us to do?'

He made sure that our hands were clean, also our finger nails. 'When the guests arrive, circulate round with trays of drinks and food. Call everyone 'sir' or 'madam.' OK lads, got that? Good.'

The guests would be arriving at any minute. The quarterdeck had been transformed; soft seats were placed round the edges of the 'dance floor', two long trestle tables had been placed on each side. These tables were laden with tasty snacks of all kinds. At the very end of the quarterdeck, a bar had been set up, with the three stewards acting as barmen. The guests began to arrive. The ladies wore long evening gowns, and the men were in uniforms. They were made up of senior officers from the dockyard, with a sprinkling of naval nurses from the base hospital, and our own officers, who began to mix with the guests.

Our Captain went to the gangway to await the arrival of the Admiral, the senior officer of the dockyard and in overall command of our flotilla, and his party. We could hear the shrill cry of the bosuns' pipes – the great man had at last arrived. With the Admiral's party was the Captain of the dockyard and his wife. Also with them – I had to look twice and was later to learn – was a girl in the uniform of a Second officer in the W.R.E.N.S. She had short blond hair, cut in a bob style, and had the bluest eyes I had ever seen. The P.O. Steward was standing close by.

'John,' I said. 'Who is that girl?'

He laughed. 'She is way out of your league, Dave.

That's her mother and father, Captain of the dockyard. She works in the signals' office ashore.' Soon she was surrounded by all the junior officers.

'What's her name, John?' I asked.

'You're keen, mate. You would not get a look in. Her name's Helen Driscoll, satisfied now?'

For the next hour I was kept busy taking round drinks and food to the guests and trying not to bump into people on the dance floor. I noticed that Helen Driscoll was also kept busy; all the officers kept asking her to dance.

As the evening progressed, the air became hot and humid and quite a lot of the junior officers were getting the worse for wear. There would be some hefty mess bills in the morning. I returned to the bar to get another tray of drinks and, sitting in the corner, out of sight, was Helen Driscoll.

'Excuse me, madam, can I get you anything?' I asked her.

'I'd give anything for a glass of iced water,' she said. 'I'm trying to keep out of the way for a bit. Those officers have trodden on my poor aching feet too often. I've been on duty all day and I'm a bit tired.' I could see she had slipped her shoes off. 'That's better,' she said. I could smell her perfume.

No wonder the officers were always around her. She had a way of looking directly at you, with those beautiful eyes. She smiled and said, 'I see you are in signals too. I may have decoded some of your traffic in the Office.' She was about twenty-two years old but looked much younger. As the P.O. Steward said, she was way out of my league.

'Can I get you anything else, ma'am?'

'Look, you don't have to keep calling me ma'am. My name is Helen,' she said. 'What's yours?'

'I'm David.' We chatted for about another ten minutes. I didn't want it to end.

'I'll regretfully have to go now before I'm missed,' she told me.

'Look, Helen', I said. 'I'll most likely be shot at dawn for saying this, but can I see you again?'

She gave me a slow smile. 'I'd like that, David.' She opened her handbag and wrote me a number down on a piece of paper. 'Call me at the office when you can.' Another slow smile and she was gone.

The Captain walked over to us and thanked us for our help. 'P.O. Steward, give the lads a drink please, they have earned it.' As he turned to go, he said to me with a smile, 'That was a very pretty girl you were talking to, Sharp. Remember she's a WREN Officer. I was young once. Better keep it quiet.' He patted me on the back and was gone. He doesn't miss a trick. I vowed that, God willing, one day I would be just like him – and anyway, I had got Helen's phone number.

Chapter Five

The Bungalow

For the next few days I was kept busy with my duties. We were due to begin our patrol within the next two weeks. One morning the Yeoman called me over. 'Dave, I want you to go over to the signals office in the dockyard to collect the codes for our forthcoming patrol. Here's your pass.'

The signal office! I thought maybe I could see Helen again. I had wanted to phone her a couple of times but I was always kept too busy. The signals office was an imposing building, four stories high, with the signal tower to one side. I went up to the sentries who were posted outside. They were armed with rifles.

'Pass, please.' The sentry had a quick look at it. 'OK, report to the desk sergeant, he will point you in the right direction.'

I showed the sergeant my pass. 'You want office one, second door on the right, top of the stairs.'

'Thanks sergeant.' I said.

I opened the door, and there sat Helen. She looked beautiful. We both tried to talk at once. In the background I could hear the busy chatter of typewriters and teleprinters.

'I tried to phone you a couple of times, but was not able to, the forthcoming patrol is very hush-hush as you know.'

'I thought you had forgotten me. I was going to phone you with some excuse so that we could talk.' She smiled in that way of hers. 'David, please don't think me awful, I'm not usually like this. I've got a short weekend leave this week. Could you get off too? I have a friend whose parents own a small bungalow right by the sea.'

'Yes, I could get away at 1200 hours Saturday,' I said.

'That's settled then,' Helen said in that direct way of hers. 'I'll meet you outside the main dockyard gates. On the way, we could stop off at the market so that you can buy some civvies, then we can blend into the background; we can just be tourists. She gave me the code books. Just then, in walked the senior signals officer. 'Signalman Sharp come to collect the code books for Salisbury, sir.'

'Make sure he signs for them.'

'Sign here, please', she said, giving me a broad wink. 'See you Saturday.' I couldn't wait!

The weekend came round at last. I stood outside the gates and noticed across the road, parked by a food stall, an old MG Sports car with Helen sitting behind the wheel.

'Hello Dave. We must have transport, jump in', she said, and off we went. She began telling me about the bungalow. It was looked after by an old retainer and his wife. It had two bedrooms and stood in its own grounds.

Helen knew her way around Singapore and we were soon at the market where I went to buy some clothes. I chose a short-sleeved shirt, some slacks, and a pair of sandals. The shopkeeper kindly let me change in the back of the shop. I came out feeling a different person. 'Suits you,' said Helen. I couldn't stop staring at her. She was wearing a bright yellow dress which matched her hair; she looked beautiful. 'Don't keep looking at me, Dave, it makes me nervous', she said, smiling that smile and giving my hand a squeeze. She was a very good driver, and we soon left Singapore far behind.

'Not long now, we should see the house when we top the next rise.' She was laughing and excited. We crested the next hill. 'Look,' she said, 'there it is.' The bungalow was nestled among the palm trees, very close to a crescent-shaped beach of pure white sand. The sea looked crystal clear. 'Do you like it, Dave?' Helen asked.

'Yes, I think it's marvellous,' I replied.

As we drew up to the front porch, the door opened and an old man came out to meet us. 'Hello again missy, and you, sir. Everything is ready for you.'

The old man's wife appeared, carrying a tray with iced cold beers on it. 'Please take,' she said. 'We hope your stay will be a very happy one.'

The bungalow had a large verandah running all the way round it, with lounge chairs dotted here and there. The only sound to be heard was the gentle lapping of the surf as it met the beach.

'Let's unpack,' Helen suggested, 'then we can have a swim and catch up on our tan.' We swam, and splashed each other like two young puppies until we were both exhausted and flopped down on the warm sand. Helen's costume was moulded to her body. I couldn't help admiring. 'You are doing it again,' she said, smiling.

We lay on the beach side by side and talked of our past lives and what we hoped for the future. Time passed far too quickly, and dusk was approaching. 'I guess we had better go inside now.' It was getting chilly. 'I'll have a shower and meet you in the lounge.' A little later, Helen came into the room. I was just pouring us a glass of wine. She was wearing a kingfisher electric blue chamsong; she looked radiant and very beautiful. I walked over to her and took her hands in mine, then put my arms around her and kissed her for the first time. She returned the kiss, and just to hold her in my arms was something I would never forget. She clung to me and I could smell the perfume again. It sent my senses reeling.

There was a discreet knock on the door. It was M-Ling, the housekeeper. 'Dinner is served, missy and sir.' He drew back the bamboo screens to reveal a low table where they had put the food. They had placed cushions on the floor for us to sit on. The meal was simple but delicious, oriental chicken with noodles, together with a bottle of the local wine to wash it down. Helen and I just sat there and talked; we were both very happy. No sign of shyness or awkwardness; we were just together, the Navy long forgotten.

After the meal we danced to the music of the gramophone and drank the rest of the wine. It was getting dark now, with the chance of rain and thunder. We kissed each other goodnight and went to our separate rooms.

Lying in bed, I could hear the raindrops beating against the windowpane. The storm seemed to be getting closer. It had been a wonderful day, one I would never forget. I was just dropping off to sleep when I heard the latch of the bedroom door opening very quietly, and the soft pat pat of feet on the floor. I opened my eyes, and there stood Helen. She didn't say a word, but let slip to the floor the night gown she was wearing. She stood like a marble statue in the light from the window. Then she pulled the sheets down and slipped into the bed beside me. We kissed and, slowly at first, explored each others' bodies. It was the first time for both of us. Whilst the thunder raged outside, all night we made love with mounting passion. As the dawn slowly lit the room, we at last fell asleep in each others' arms.

Later that day, Helen and I said goodbye to this idyllic place. Helen held my hand and said, 'You will be careful when you leave on this patrol. You see, I know where you are going.'

The old retainer and his wife waved us off. 'Come back soon, missy and sir. I so glad for you. You are happy here.'

We soon arrived back in Singapore, and Helen dropped me two streets away from the dockyard gates so that we wouldn't have to answer any awkward questions. I changed into my uniform and reported back on board.

'Had a good weekend, Dave?' the lads asked. I smiled. If they only knew, I thought; but I knew Helen would be waiting when we got back from patrol.

Chapter Six

The Patrol

We had left Singapore, and had been at sea now for two weeks. Nothing of any interest had occurred. At a steady 10 knots we made our way up the straits. The only company we had were the flying fish, skimming across the waves and, one day, the shape of a giant ray sailing serenely below us. The ship's normal routine went on until the evening of the sixteenth day at sea.

'Radar, Bridge, echo bearing 025 degrees; range 3 miles, can you make it out?' enquired the Captain.

'It looks like a small fishing boat, sir,' replied Lt Pringle, who was the officer of the watch. 'I don't think it is anything to worry about, sir. Shall we carry on with our normal course, sir?'

'Our orders are to stop and investigate any vessels. Stand by to lower the motor whaler with a boarding party. I want them armed with lanchesters. Get on with it Pringle', the Captain ordered. 'Radar, Bridge, what's it look like now, Forbes?' He was the senior operator on board, and very good at his job.

'Bearing the same, sir. Range now 2 miles.'

'Very good. Increase to 100 revolutions; muster the boarding party,' the Captain called. 'Lookouts, keep on your toes, we should spot it soon.'

'Ship at action stations, sir,' said the gunnery officer (not bad, we did it in two minutes flat). A rain squall had come up, but in the distance we could just make out the vessel.

'Looks like a fishing boat, sir,' Yeo Pole reported. 'It looks as though it's been on fire.' As we got closer, we could smell the smoke. She is very low down by the bows. We were now only 400 yards away and coming up to her on the port side. I was to go with the boarding party as the signalman and report back to the ship.

'Lt Pringle, you are officer in charge; I want you to bring back any charts, ship's papers, or other documents you can find.'

We scrambled into the sea boat, slip, and we were away. As we neared the fishing boat, the strong smell of burning and charred wood came wafting over us. It was indeed a native fishing boat, badly down by the bows and in danger of sinking at any minute. We could see no sign of life on board. There was just an eerie silence.

Lt Pringle said, 'We'll get on board and have a quick look around and get back to the ship.' He made to clamber on board.

'I think we should board from the other side,' said P.O. gunner. 'If our ship has to open fire we would be in the way.'

'Well, if you think so P.O.,' said Pringle. He should have thought of that himself. We threw grapnels over the bulwarks and scrambled aboard. It was deathly quiet; the only sound we could hear was the gurgling of sea water coming into the vessel deep in the bows. We approached the wheelhouse. It was badly shot up, a long line of bullet holes ran along the rear of the structure. The bullet-ridden body of the helmsman lay huddled on the deck by the wheel, covered in blood. Lt Pringle was deathly pale. 'Come on, hurry up and let's get back to the ship', he said.

'Sir, the Captain said to look for any papers or charts. I'll have a look down below.' I went down the ladder into the hold; it was dark and smelled of stale fish and diesel oil. Slumped in the corner were two bodies of the crew. They hadn't been dead very long. They had been shot to pieces. The remains of a meal lay on a rackety table. The small cabin had been ransacked. Whoever they were, what had they been looking for? Arms or drugs? Lt Pringle by this time was getting very nervous. The vessel gave another lurch.

'She's going, quick, back to the ship,' he shouted. We quickly went over the side and returned to the ship.

As we turned away from the ill-fated fishing boat, it was as though she was very tired. She finally slipped beneath the waves, taking the bodies of her dead crew with her, whoever they were.

The Captain called us to the bridge. 'Well, report?' he asked Lt Pringle.

'Nothing found, sir,' he said. 'Three dead crewmen. She's been on fire and is sinking.'

'Very well, Pilot, make a report to Base; give a sighting latitude and longitude and our position. We shall resume our original course and carry on with the patrol.'

As he turned to leave the bridge, I said, 'Excuse me sir, I found these on the bodies of the crewmen. They look like dog-tags and some sort of Pay book.'

The Captain looked at them. 'These are issued to communist troops. Good work, Sharp; thank God somebody has some sense. I'll put it in my report.'

Lt Pringle hurried down to his cabin, ignoring the puzzled looks of the seamen as he sped past. He sat down at his desk, his hands were shaking badly as he reached into the bottom drawer and took out the stored bottle of gin. He took a couple of deep swigs. 'I can't go on like this any more.' He could picture in his mind's eye the dead blood-stained bodies of the Malay fishermen, the smell of burning, and of the ship sinking; also the looks of the sea boat's crew. 'I'm not cut out for this kind of life. I must get off this bloody ship.' He took another swallow of the neat gin to get away from the mocking looks of his fellow officers. He could taste the sour vomit in the back of his throat, and was violently sick in the hand basin.

And so we carried on with our patrol; long days and nights, 4 hours on duty, and 4 hours off. So it went on. We did have a few bright moments, usually on a Sunday. One of them as I remember was, 'Hands to bathe.' If the radar gave us a clear picture, the ship was stopped and the ship's whaler was lowered, manned by a crew of four. One of the lads was armed with a lanchester machine gun, just in case the sharks became too nosy, and got too close. Those of us who were not on watch could dive into the water; it was so refreshing to get away from the ship for a short time and to relax. One of the other interludes was a Banyan (a picnic) on some remote island where it was safe to anchor. It allowed us to go ashore for a few hours. The ship's cooks prepared us some sandwiches and we were allowed to take our beer ration ashore with us. We had a great time exploring the island and swimming in the clear water. As we dived under, we could see all the tropical fish and the beautiful formations of the coral on the sea bottom. Georgie said to me as we lay on the sand, 'You know what, Dave, the folks back home would pay hundreds of pounds to have a chance of this.' I could only agree.

Today was a Red Letter Day – aircraft from our base in Singapore dropped our mail, and yes, I had four letters from Helen. She said how much she missed me and couldn't wait for us to return to the bungalow. It would be a few weeks yet. Mail from home too; some good news, some bad. Some of the lads received 'Dear John letters', mostly from well-intentioned people. For example, 'Just thought I would let you know that while you have been away I could not help noticing your wife has been entertaining gentlemen friends until the early hours. Just thought I would let you know...'

Our Leading Telegraphist, Pete Noble, had become a dad – mother and baby daughter both doing well. We couldn't get cigars, but it was tots all round, with a hell of a party once we returned to base.

This will give you some idea of how we passed the time on our patrol. We got to know each other very well, living in a close community such as ours.

We had been on patrol now for eight weeks and had not sighted another vessel. One morning, I was sitting in the mess enjoying a cup of stand-easy coffee when I heard over the tannoy: 'Signalman Sharp, report to the Captain's cabin.' I grabbed my cap and thought, 'what have I done now?' I knocked on his door.

'Come in.' As I entered, the Captain was sitting behind his desk, and also present was my Divisional Officer.

'You wanted to see me, sir?'

'Yes, Sharp. Don't look so worried. Your promotion to Leading Signalman has come through, and has been approved.' We shook hands. 'Well done,' he said, and gave me my hook to sew on to my uniform.

When I returned to the mess, the lads asked me what it was all about. I laughed and said, 'Listen you lot, I want a bit more respect around here now,' and showed them my new hook. They gave me a lot of good-natured ribbing. 'Come round at tot time, Hooky, glad you made it.'

As the days passed, the weather began to get worse. Gone were the gentle swells. Black storm clouds began to gather. We could see on the horizon heavy rain squalls creeping towards us. The sea itself changed colour; it was now a dirty pewter mixture. The wind had got up to gale force; we could feel the ship rolling in a sickening corkscrew motion. Lightning lit up the sky overhead; then it began to rain, not just a soft downpour, but a deluge of water. We on the bridge had no protection at all as it was an open bridge and subject to anything the weather could throw at us. The air was humid and sticky. Underneath our oilskins we could feel the sweat running down our backs. The Monsoon Season had arrived.

Looking back, the dark days seemed to blend into each

other. We were constantly on the lookout for any suspicious vessels. Riding through this type of weather didn't help us much. Tempers began to flare up. We were all hoping for our recall back to Singapore. The Captain had arranged for us to re-fuel at sea. We were to meet up with RNA Black Ranger (the fleet tanker and supply ship), the next day. Halfway through the morning watch, the senior P.O. Tel came up to the Bridge with an urgent signal for the Captain. He quickly read the signal. 'Call a meeting of all the officers in the plot room in ten minutes, except the officer of the watch. I would like the doctor to attend also, quick as you can,' he said.

I asked Yeo what this was all about. 'We'll find out soon enough. I'm going below for my tot, you can go for yours when I come back. Keep your eye on the plot room, call me if anything happens.'

At last I managed to get to the mess to have my tot and to try to dry out a little, when an announcement came over the tannoy: 'The following ratings report to the plot room right away. Able Seaman Honor, White, Reynolds, Roberts, Peterson, Leading Signalman Sharp, and Sick berth attendant Wallace.' What was this all about?

On our entry to the plot room, Lt Pringle, the ship's doctor, the navigating officer, and the Captain met us. 'As you know I have had a top action signal from base. We have been asked to go to the assistance of five Nuns and approximately seventy-five children who are trapped in a mission about eleven miles inland. They are all French. Our job is to take them out, get them back to the ship and evacuate them to Singapore as quickly as possible. The communist troops are closing in and they are in danger of being cut off. The Army can't help; they are too far away and can't get there in time. This is what I propose to do – I shall put a landing party ashore, which will be made up of you. The navigator says that if we put on full steam, we can be there in about six hours. We have been told by the Army that there is a path of sorts leading up to the mission; it's likely to be overgrown in places so you will have to expect anything.' Lt Pringle will be in overall charge, together with the doctor.

You will all be armed with rifles, and, as an added precaution, you will take some plastic explosives. You will have rations for twenty-four hours and, of course, first aid kits. Are there any questions? Sharp, you will carry ship to shore radio and keep us informed at all times. It's now 1230 hours, muster by the sea boat at 1800 hours with your arms and equipment. One last word,' he said, 'the communist troops have been attacking the planters and killing owners, men, women, and children, and destroying any buildings, so time is of the essence. The mission is sited by a village called Wey Saign, eleven miles from where we can drop you off. Good luck to you all.'

Chapter Seven

The Mission

After six hours of hard steaming we came to the position on the chart, a small bay with a safe anchorage. We dropped anchor about half a mile from a gently shelving beach where we were to land. Close by was a deserted village. The path we were to take could clearly be seen. We landed. 'Right, let's go', said Lt Pringle. He appeared to be in a very agitated state of mind and was shouting unnecessary, meaningless orders.

The doctor said to Lt Pringle, 'Don't you think it would be a good idea to place someone in front of us to be on the lookout for an ambush? We're wide open here.'

'OK Sharp, see to it.' I would have thought that Pringle should have thought of it himself.

'Taff,' I said, 'Go about 200 yards ahead of us and keep a good lookout.'

'You know what, Dave, there's a rumour going round that Pringle hasn't got a mother!'

'Stow it, Taff. If he hears you he'll have you on a charge,' I advised. We set off. 'I'll radio the ship, doctor, and let them know we are on our way. Is that OK, sir?'

'Yes. Please go ahead.'

The pathway was overgrown with creepers and undergrowth. We had to hack our way through. It was still raining, and the air was hot and humid. The only sounds we could hear were the chatter of the monkeys and birds. As we made our way through, I could see Lt Pringle was already beginning to feel the strain. We had only been on the march for an hour.

He was talking to the Doctor. 'I'm not at all sure about this,' he said. 'The Army should have got them out.' I was rapidly beginning to have doubts about him; he was supposed to be in charge of us and tell us what to do. At least the rain had stopped. Steam rose from the jungle floor. We were all wet through with the rain and our own sweat. The straps of the radio were beginning to cut into my shoulders. We had marched for about eight miles now, passing over the only bridge spanning the river. We wondered how it managed to keep up. We could plainly see that it had not been used for a long time. It was now beginning to get dark as it only can in the jungle – one minute daylight, the next pitch blackness. The doctor and Lt Pringle went into a huddle.

'I think it would be a good idea for us to take a short break now. It will begin to get light about 04.30 in the morning and we will be able to see where we are going.'

'We had better post some watches, sir,' I suggested.

'Good thinking.' Pringle should have thought of this as well. Any respect I might have had for him was quickly disappearing. It was not right for the doctor to have to think of these things. I split the lads up into watches, an hour for each of us. We would make an early start in the morning. According to the map, the Mission was only about five miles away now, so we settled down, trying to find a dry spot on the jungle floor and making sure there was nothing nasty lurking close by.

At first light we started off. As we advanced along the jungle path, we could hear gun fire in the distance. It seemed to be getting closer. Taffy came running back down the path towards us.

'We have arrived, I can see the Mission,' he said.

As we approached, we could see the buildings were all white in the reflected sunlight. The central structure was a bell tower of sorts, with many outbuildings. All round the Mission ran an eight-foot high wall, made from local stone, with two massive wooden front gates, firmly shut. A huge bell was positioned over the gates. We rang it and it seemed to echo and vibrate all around us.

We shouted, 'Don't be afraid, it's the Navy. We have come to help you.'

Slowly the huge doors opened. 'Thank God you've come. I was beginning to give up all hope. My name is Sister Mary; I am the Mother Superior here, and these are the Sisters, Anne, Jane, and Ruby. I'm afraid they only speak a little English. We are a French Order; our Parish Priest, Father Donald, passed away two months ago and we have been on our own since then. I have managed to work the radio and asked for help. These are the children.'

They were all seated on the ground, the elder ones caring for the younger ones. They were a mixture of Malay, Indian, and a few Europeans. A lot of them looked in a pretty bad way. Our doctor soon got to work. We had to get them ready for our return trip to the ship. They all looked hungry and some of them, according to the doctor, were in the first stages of beri-beri. A lot of them were suffering from malnutrition.

The distant sounds of gunfire were getting much closer. 'For God's sake, hurry up,' said Lt Pringle. 'We must get out of here.'

'We shall go when I am good and ready,' replied the doctor, 'and not before! Sharp.' He asked me to radio the ship and let them know we were on our way back. The children, we could see, were getting very frightened. The Nuns formed them up into two rows, the elder ones carrying the younger ones. We also carried a child; I was toting a little Malay girl who, according to Sister Mary, had stepped on a thorn and it had turned her foot septic. The good doctor bandaged it up for her. All the children had name tags, which they wore around their necks. My little girl was called Mi Ling; she clung on tightly. You could see the absolute trust in their eyes. They must have been through hell for children so young.

We and the Nuns started off on our return journey, the Nuns helping the children along. The Nuns' once white habits were now getting muddy and soiled. The rain continued to fall, but we pressed on. Still the gunfire persisted, and it was getting closer.

The Nuns were marvellous; they kept encouraging the children. 'It's not too far now, we'll soon be there,' they were saying. Sister Mary tried to speak to us in English but was finding it a little hard.

'Now try not to worry, everything will turn out all right,' encouraged the doctor.

Lt Pringle came puffing up. 'We must hurry, if some of the children can't go any faster we shall have to leave them behind. This is madness. The communist forces will soon be here and you know what they do to captured prisoners.'

He was now really getting on my nerves. 'If someone doesn't shut him up, he will get a smack on the jaw from me. He's supposed to lead us, but look at him.'

'I agree with you, but he's not worth a court martial. At the end of the mission, it would give me the greatest satisfaction to shut him up, officer or no officer. He shouldn't be wearing the uniform.'

We had now been on the march for four hours. It was very slow going and we had left the Mission far behind. Taff came running up to me. 'Don't tell the others, but they must have set the mission on fire. You can see the smoke behind us.'

'How far behind us do you think they are, Taff?' I enquired.

'No more than two miles, I reckon.'

We were only a few yards away from the bridge now. The rifle fire was getting very much closer. 'Doctor,' I said, 'You and the Nuns take the children across. Taff and I will stay this side to cover you. I'll radio the ship to let them know you are on your way.'

By this time, the children were getting very tired. We kept trying to cajole them. 'It's not very far now, you will soon have plenty to eat and drink.' The Nuns were a tower of strength, with never a word of complaint and always ready to help.

Lt Pringle again called, 'Hurry! Hurry! You must all hurry.' At that moment, mortar fire began to fall around us. 'Quickly, get the children away.' They were tired by now, and terrified. We all made our way across the bridge.

I said to Pringle – I had no more respect for him at all now – 'You go back with the others. I'm going to blow up the bridge. It will hold the communist troops up and give us a chance to get back to the ship.'

'If you think it's right, I'll go with the others.' He ran off. Thank God for that, I thought. The bridge, made up of rickety logs taken from the jungle trees, was embedded into the sides of the gorge. It was about five feet wide and held in place by ropes, slung across a now raging torrent below, owing to the Monsoon rains up country.

As Taff and I scrambled down the sides of the embankment to lay the charges, we came under rifle fire from the other side. We would have to be quick. We lay the plastic charges and primed the fuses; we had just one minute to get clear. As we crawled back up the bank I felt a needle sharp pain in the calf of my left leg.

'Are you OK?' asked Taff.

'Just a nick in the leg.'

As we flung ourselves down, there was a terrific explosion behind us. When the dust had settled, we saw we had knocked out the centre span of the bridge; about fifteen feet was gone.

'That will hold the bastards up for a bit. Now let's get the hell out of here,' I said to Taff. At last we came to the inlet, and the ship's boat was waiting for us. What a welcome sight! We were very tired and dirty.

As we clambered aboard, the P.O. Steward was waiting for us with a tot of rum. 'Captain's orders. Drink up, then go to the sickbay to get yourselves fixed up. The Captain will send for you shortly. The Nuns and the children are all quite safe. The doctor is looking after them, and Sister Mary has been in touch with the people in Singapore.'

Two hours later I was reporting to the Captain. As I knocked on his door, I tried to remember all that had happened in the past two days.

'Come in.' The Captain was sitting behind his desk as usual. 'How are you feeling?' he asked me, 'and how's the leg?'

'I'm fine sir, it's just a scratch. The doctor took care of it.'

The Captain looked at me with his piercing blue eyes. 'The doctor has given me a full report, and has explained what was happening. Now, as regards the bridge, (now I'm for it, I thought), if I were placed in the same position as you, I would have done exactly the same as you did. But for your quick thinking we might not have got everyone safely back to Singapore. We are now steaming at full speed back to base and should arrive there at 1600 tomorrow. Well done! Now go and get some rest, you have earned it.'

But first I went to see the children and the Nuns. I found them in high spirits and enjoying the attention they were receiving. They were stuffing themselves with NAAFI chocolate, fruit, and cakes. Mi-Ling gave me a special big hug. I said my goodbyes until tomorrow and went back to the mess deck. I couldn't help wondering what the Captain had said to Lt Pringle.

Right on time, we arrived back at our base in Singapore. There was quite a reception committee waiting for us, and two buses to take the children and the Nuns back to the Children's Home. They went down the gangway clutching as much chocolate and sweets as they could carry, with the cheers of our crew ringing in their ears. We had grown quite attached to them over the past few days and we wished them God speed. There was quite a crowd milling about on the jetty, together with a group of senior Officers waiting to come aboard. As we looked on, two medical officers came aboard and escorted Lt Pringle off the ship into a waiting ambulance. I could not help feeling sorry for him. His naval career was at an end.

Now all I wanted was to make a phone call to Helen. At 1800 hours she was waiting for me in her little car outside the dockyard gates. We spent a very happy time saying hello in a small back street Chinese restaurant, holding hands. I plucked up the courage and asked her to marry me. She said yes. 'We will have a few problems to sort out, darling,' I said. 'Not the least, your parents.'

'Don't worry. I'll arrange a meeting with Daddy. He's very sweet really. All too soon the weekend leave was over and I had to return to the ship. Helen said she would phone me when she had arranged a meeting with her parents.

I had only been back on board for about an hour when an announcement over the tannoy called me once again to the Captain's cabin. I knocked on the door.

'Come in.' The Captain was with my Divisional Officer (now what had I done?) 'Hello, Sharp, had a good weekend?' he asked

'Yes thank you, sir,' I replied, wondering if anyone had found out about Helen and me.

'On Wednesday we have to go over to see the French Ambassador at the French Embassy. It gives me great pleasure to tell you that you have been awarded the Croix-de-Guerre for services rendered. You have also been mentioned in dispatches, along with all the others in the landing party.'

One week later we were back on patrol and only searched five vessels, nothing found. Six weeks later, our patrol ended and we returned to Singapore.

Chapter Eight

Admiralty House

Helen and I spent a wonderful weekend at the bungalow again, where we celebrated my 22nd birthday. It was August now and our spell of duty was nearly at an end. I knew all the lads would be pleased to return home to their wives and families once again. But what of Helen and me? Her father, I knew, would soon be retiring from the Service at Christmas, and was going to buy a smallholding in Kent – to set up a market-garden business – and enjoy his retirement.

Helen had arranged a meeting with her parents for the following Saturday at Admiralty House. I was a bag of nerves to say the least. No matter which way you looked at it, her father was still the Captain of the Dockyard here in Singapore, and I was just a lowly rating.

As Saturday was fast approaching, I kept myself busy with my duties on board the ship. I was just writing up the latest signals log when the tannoy once again told me to report to the Captain's cabin. (They must have found out about Helen and me). Now I'm for it, I thought. I knocked on his door and entered.

'Come in and sit down, David.' It was the first time he had called me by my Christian name. 'I just want to ask you a few questions. How would you feel about taking a commission?' he asked me. I was totally unprepared for this. 'Your service record is excellent; you have been highly recommended for this by all your superiors. It would mean you would have to fly home shortly and begin to do the four months' Officer's training course at HMS King Alfred, because you have come from the lower deck, which is not unheard of these days.'

'When would I have to leave, sir?' I asked him.

'Well, if you agree it will be in about two weeks' time, once I have set the wheels in motion.' He smiled. 'I think you must have a few loose ends to tie up ashore.' I was in a daze – this was a dream come true.

'Yes sir,' I replied, 'I would be very happy to accept a commission if I can manage to pass the exams.'

'I'm very pleased to hear it, David. I'll put the wheels in motion right away. I shall be very sorry to lose you. Within the service, as you will no doubt find out, it is like a very small family, and somewhere along the line we will meet again.' With that he shook hands and that was that! I just hoped that one day I would be just like him.

I phoned Helen to tell her the good news, and we arranged to meet at the same place, same time. This was the big event for me, meeting her mother and father for the first time. I wondered just what kind of reception I would get. It was a strict rule within the service, no (repeat, no) liaisons with WREN Officers unless of equal rank. Saturday eventually came round. I met Helen at the usual place. I must admit I was very nervous at meeting her parents for the first time.

'Now don't worry, darling,' she said, 'I've told them all about you.'

'I'm still worried.'

'You will soon be an officer, so what's the harm?' As we drove up to Admiralty House, past the magnificent black wrought-iron gates, along the long sweeping driveway bedecked with flower beds, and up to the main entrance, I thought I'll have to get a grip on myself. Helen gave my hand a squeeze. Outside the main door stood two armed naval sentries. 'Evening miss,' one of them said. They gave me a good looking over, quite uncertain what to do about me. 'Er, good evening,' he said to me in a questionable voice. Helen took my hand and we went inside this beautiful building.

The whole place seemed to glow, polished floors, a deep red carpet ran the whole way along the entrance hall; gold and tapestry, guilt tables and chairs lined the walls. Pictures of naval battles and past events were hung on the walls each side. Now for it, I thought. A side door opened.

'Hello David, I'm Helen's mother. I've heard so much about you.' We shook hands; she had a way about her that made you feel at ease right away, a very charming lady. 'Peter will be down shortly. Helen, show David into the lounge, please do sit down.'

By this time my hands were shaking. I was beginning to feel very out of place, and wished I was back on the ship. Just then the door opened. 'Hello, David, Helen's father. Please relax, don't look so worried. Would you like a drink? I think we could all use one. Helen, do the honours please.' We got our drinks. I was beginning to feel a little more relaxed. 'Let's sit down and talk. I understand from Helen you two want to get married?'

'I do, sir,' I replied. I was finding this really tough going. I began to explain to him about my forthcoming promotion.

'Yes, David, I know all about that. I have had a word with your commanding officer. I'll tell you now, David, I've never seen Helen so happy. If she is happy, then so are we. Go ahead with our blessing. As Helen may have told you, I shall be leaving the Service shortly. We have bought a smallholding in Kent. This will be my last appointment before we fly home.'

We all four of us talked for a further hour. I liked this man, my future father-in-law, very down to earth. I knew we would get on well. 'I knew you would like them,' Helen said, taking my hand. 'Let's go into dinner.' The meal was very informal, and we talked about everything under the sun, from our hopes for the future to the price of vegetables for the market-garden. When we entered the dining room, a table of highly polished mahogany ran the length of the room, with twelve matching chairs. In the centre of the table was a candelabra, holding candles to match. It was all very impressive; overhead the gentle sound of the spinning fans. At the rear of the room was a large beautiful antique drinks cabinet. I could not help admiring it.

'Yes, it's grand isn't it, David?'

'Where did you manage to get it?' I asked.

'I picked it up in Hong Kong a couple of years ago. I shall be taking it home with us when we leave.' The dinner was served by the Malay house-boys, and was delicious. We all spent a very pleasant evening together, chatting away. I was sorry when it was time for me to leave these nice people. As I kissed Helen goodnight, she said, 'Mum and Dad like you. They are going to write to your Mum and tell her all about us,' which I thought was very nice of them.

'Well I guess they know all about us on the ship now, including the Captain.'

She looked at me with that knowing look of hers. 'I wish we were back at the bungalow right now.'

'So do I, darling, but I have to get back to the ship. I am on duty in the morning. I shall have to start packing my gear, ready for my flight back to the UK. I'll see you again on Sunday, same place, same time.' We took our time saying our good nights, and I returned to the ship.

Sunday, my last night in Singapore. My kit was all packed ready to go. Helen and I met, and we had supper at Admiralty House. Afterwards, Helen and I said our goodbyes, this time until Christmas when she would be leaving the Service to help to manage the smallholding in Kent. We promised to write every day, hugged each other, and said a tearful goodbye. It will soon be Christmas and then we will be together again.

The next day I said goodbye to all my friends on board. We had been together for two years and had been through a lot together. It was a sad wrench, but knowing the Navy, we would one day all meet up again. I had the usual good natured ribbing. 'Officer! I've shot 'em,' and 'You won't get me to salute you.'

It was all taken in good fun from men like these you could rely on.

The Captain called me to his cabin once again. I thanked him for all he had done for me and we shook hands. 'Good luck, David. I expect the next time we meet you will have a little gold braid on your arm. I would be very pleased to have you under my command again in the future.'

The transport came to take me to the airport. I was on my way. What would Royal Alfred hold in store for me, I wondered? It would be a long flight home. I would always treasure the time I had spent in Singapore, and that little piece of Heaven, the bungalow by the beach, and all the true friends I had made along the way.

As I boarded the aircraft, I could see the little white sports car parked by the perimeter fence, and Helen waving me off. As we became airborne, I tried to see the ship in the dockyard. Yes, there she was, a tiny midget, distorted by the sun's rays and the heat haze. She had been my home for so long. I'll never forget her. As we climbed higher and higher, Singapore was lost in the distance and all I could see were the clouds.

Chapter Nine

HMS King Alfred

From the bus, which had driven us from the railway station, we got the first glimpse of King Alfred. In the centre was a mansion of the old country period, set in its own grounds. In front, where once would have been landscaped gardens, was the parade ground, with a painted white flag pole flying the white Ensign, showing it to be a naval establishment. On each side of the entrance were curved stone steps with a long sweeping balcony going right across the front of the building. From where we were standing, we could see a football pitch, tennis courts, and cricket pitches. Hopefully we'd have plenty of time for the sport of our choice. There were ten of us in our group: Chief Petty Officers, Petty Officers, and Leading Hands, like me. The bus parked outside the main entrance. The driver, who was an old Navy pensioner, said, 'This way, please gentlemen.'

We followed him inside and put our suitcases down. What an impressive place this was! There was a long winding staircase going up both sides of the entrance hall. A door opened at the side of the lobby. 'Good evening, gentlemen.' It was a full Commander. 'My name is

Commander Gibbs, and while you are here I shall be your Commanding Officer. You have all been highly recommended or you wouldn't be here. I would like to take this brief session to welcome you to King Alfred. Whilst you are here, all the staff will call you Sir. Your lecturers are all senior Lt Commanders. Are there any questions any of you would like to ask at this point? No? Thank you, gentlemen. The stewards will now show you to your cabins and give you time to settle in. Dinner will be served in the dining room at 1900 hours. There is a bar next to the dining room, which you can use and get to know each other. One final word. During your stay with us you will be closely monitored. That's all for now. We shall meet again tomorrow on the parade ground at 0900 hours. Good night, gentlemen.' And with that, he left us to it.

A steward showed me to my cabin, which was on the third floor. 'Here you are, sir,' the steward said. 'Hope you will be comfortable.'

It contained a bed, wardrobe, and a chest of drawers; a desk stood by the window. It looked very inviting; a bit different to the confines of the mess deck. They even did our laundry every Tuesday morning. All of us spent a very nice evening in the bar, getting to know one another. We swapped our experiences. It had been a long day and I was ready for bed. It seemed it would be quite an adventure being here and having so much to learn.

The next morning at 0900 hours on the dot, we fell in on the parade ground in our classes. Altogether there were only 100 of us who would be officers at any one time passing out, so the class was small. Our instructor was Lt

Commander Marshall, who introduced himself. We then marched to our lecture room.

'Good morning, gentlemen.' I still couldn't get used to being called 'gentlemen'. 'I'll just bring you up to date with our forthcoming programme. We shall be studying the rudiments of navigation, which is essential for your watch keeping certificates. We shall be looking at naval history. You will also be taught OLQ (Officer-like qualities), how to fit into the Wardroom, Mess bills, etc. I would advise you all to listen very carefully to your lectures and put all your effort into your studies. We are a little different here, although loosely based on the Dartmouth Naval College. As you know, their entrants usually come from Public Schools, with a Direct Entry to Dartmouth as Midshipmen. We here are somewhat of a "one off". We have all come from the lower deck, where hard work and experience have paid off. Hopefully you can teach the younger members of the Navy something useful. You wouldn't be here otherwise.'

The three months seemed to be flying by, day and night swotting for our exams to follow shortly. The conversation in the bar that night was all about whether we could pass.

We had now been in Royal Alfred for two months. This was the week I had been looking forward to. We were to join a fleet minesweeper, HMS Raven, a ship which was used by the Navy to teach us young up-and-coming-would-be officers about ship handling, navigation and seamanship. We were to travel to Portland Naval Base by coaches.

At last, after a long trip, stopping for the lads to go to the toilet, etc, we arrived. As we drew alongside the ship,

I was impressed by the look of her, decked out in her new paint, flying a brand new Ensign; she was beautiful to my eyes. She was 150 feet long; bt 18 foot beam; a squat funnel, and a short mast which carried all wireless lines, etc. We were to live and work in her for the next week, under the watchful eye of Lt Cdr Marshall. I think everyone was a little nervous at this point; this was it, no going back. A little gold braid on your arm; can you hack it or not? There is much more to being an officer than having the uniform on. As we gathered on the tiny quarterdeck, Lt Cdr Marshall was very busy writing on his log sheet. 'Listen, all of you,' he said. 'Tomorrow morning we shall take the ship to sea. We shall carry out various exercises whilst under way and then return to harbour. Are there any questions? No? Very good. We shall meet here on the quarterdeck at 0630 in the morning.

'Right, who will be first to take us out to sea? Any takers?' said Lt Cdr Marshall. Everyone was a little nervous at this point.

'I'll do it, sir,' I said. I was itching to have a go. After all those months on the signal deck, watching and listening, I had picked up quite a lot.

'Up to the bridge then, Sharp. I'll be in the background if you need me.' He was still busy writing on his clip board, no doubt making an assessment of my efforts. 'Just one thing to remember, pay all respects to other vessels we pass, and leave the harbour. She's all yours, carry on.'

'Boatswains mate,' I called. 'Pipe hands to stations for leaving harbour, special sea duty men close up.' I crossed to the voice pipes. 'Engine room, stand by to obey, telegraphs, stand by.' I could see about 300 yards away was a cruiser. I would have to be careful. Under my feet I could feel the gentle throb of the engines; we were all set. I moved to the centre of the bridge, pulled my cap down firmly, took a deep breath and thought 'here goes'.

'Signalman, ask the signal tower permission to proceed.' A diamond bright light flashed us, 'Proceed when ready.' 'Thank you, acknowledge.' In the eyes of the ship, I could see the duty signalman ready to haul down the Union flag as soon as we cast off, and out of the corner of my eye I saw the Admiralty Tug standing by to give assistance if needed. I leant over the side of the bridge and shouted, 'Take in breast ropes and springs.' I got a wave to tell me all was clear. 'Let go forward. Slow ahead port engine; slow astern starboard engine.' Slowly the bows began to swing clear of the jetty. 'Stop both engines, just a touch astern now, let go aft.' We were clear. 'Port 10,' I told the wheel house. '10 of port wheel, sir.' I aimed for the centre of the harbour, and as we drew level with the cruiser I called, 'Attention on the upper deck, face to port.' We were saluting our betters. The quartermaster piped the still. As she towered above us, I could see her officers looking down at us. She answered us, the Royal Marine sounded the still on the bugle. So far so good. 'Wheelhouse; bridge coxswain,' I said, 'steer straight for the harbour entrance.' He was a very experienced rating and knew exactly what to do. I felt it was no good giving unnecessary helm orders.

As we passed the harbour entrance, we could feel the first gentle rollers of the open sea coming to meet us. 'Pilot,' I said, 'Course to steer is 285 degrees.' I knew the course by heart. I had had a good look at the chart, but I wanted to let Lt Cdr Marshall know that I was on the ball. I bent to the voice pipe again. 'Full ahead both engines Wheelhouse Starboard 15.' '15 of starboard wheel on, sir', came back the reply. 'Steer 305.' I was checking the compass all the time. 'Boatswains mate, pipe fall out harbour stations, carry on with your work.' I felt a tap on my shoulder. It was Lt Cdr Marshall.

'That was nicely carried out Sharp, well done.'

I was in seventh heaven; this is where I wanted to be. For the rest of that eventful day we practiced various exercises – away seaboat crew, man overboard, and all kinds of evolutions. It was now time for us to return to harbour.

'OK, Sharp, you brought us out, now you can take us in,' said Lt Cdr Marshall. I want you to place the ship as we were this morning, bows pointing out to sea-ward.'

Once again I climbed to the Bridge. 'Boatswains mate, pipe hands to stations for entering harbour.' We passed the entrance. 'Both engines slow ahead.' I was nicely in the centre of the Channel. I decided to go about four ships lengths up the waterway to give me enough sea room to turn the vessel. 'Stop engines,' I said. The way began to fall off her. 'Port 20 Midships steady.' We were nicely angling into the jetty. 'Slow ahead port engine.' The bow was now in position. 'Stop port.' The seaman threw the heaving line to the waiting dockyard workers on the jetty and they made it fast to the bollard. 'Slow astern starboard engine.' The stern swung gently into the wall and was made fast to the stern bollard. 'Out breast and spring ropes,' I said. I rang down and said, 'Finished with main engines.'

I had done it; a feeling of intense satisfaction and pride came over me. I stood in the centre of the now deserted bridge, and as I lit my pipe, I vowed that one day I would have a command of my own. The little Admiralty tug gave a cheery toot on her whistle and went puffing back up the harbour; her services were not required.

I was looking forward to tomorrow; the same little tug would be towing a target for us to fire our guns on the firing range. Some of my fellow classmates were finding all this ship handling a little strange. This was understandable as we all came from different parts of the ship, but we all had to try. That night we all piled into taxis and had a good run ashore in Weymouth. We had to wear civilian dress, but a good time was had by all.

The next morning we put to sea once again and met up with the tug. We all had a go at controlling the guns, and when the exercise was over the tug signalled us, 'I won't play with you any more, you are getting too good.' We felt very pleased.

The next day we had to say goodbye to HMS Raven. It was time to return to Royal Alfred. I had learnt a lot from that little ship which I hoped would stand me in good stead for the future. I knew one thing for sure, I wanted a command of my own, no matter what size. It made me all the more determined.

The following day was Tuesday and we all gathered in the lecture room to hear our exam results. These were read out by Lt Cdr Marshall. There was a lot of tension in the air that morning. Our whole future in the Royal Navy depended on the results. 'Well gentlemen. I am very pleased to inform you that you have all passed.' What a relief! I had managed to pass with 94%, not a bad effort. 'I have one piece of advice for you all,' said Lt Cdr Marshall, and it has always stuck in my memory. 'The sailors will always show proper marks of respect for the uniform, but to gain proper respect, you have to earn it. Try to remember that. Now to more pleasant news; Foster & Sons, Naval Tailors, will be on hand tomorrow to supply and fit you with your new uniforms. The Passing Out Parade will be this coming Saturday at 1000 hours, so those of you who wish to invite guests may do so. A buffet will be laid on in the dining rooms after the Parade.'

Saturday – the great day had arrived. We were all dressed up in our new uniforms and felt very proud of ourselves. With the band of the Royal Marines leading, we marched on to the parade ground. Helen had come, together with her parents, and so had my mother. What a feeling of pride. I had made it to the first step on the ladder. I kept thinking back to that cold winter morning, standing on the station platform as a boy of fifteen, going to join the Navy at HMS Ganges. I wondered what the future would hold in store for me.

But that's another story.

Epilogue

On a bright sunny morning in April, Helen and I were married in the little church on the hill in the village of Westernhanger, near Sellinge in Kent. It was a truly naval occasion with most of our friends there. I had my stag night in the village pub, The Black Bull.

Our wedding reception was held in a marquee on the rear lawn of the house. As the telegrams were read out by our best man, one in particular stands out in my mind. It said, 'Good luck to you both and very best wishes from Commander Poole.' The captain of my old ship HMS Salisbury. He did not forget.

Helen and I spent a wonderful ten days on the island of Jersey in the Channel Isles for our honeymoon, and talked of our future life together and our time spent in Singapore and of the little bungalow where we had been so happy.

Glossary

Aloft – up the rigging

Berth – mooring on the wharf or jetty

Cabin – bedroom

Chief petty officer – senior non-commissioned officer

Coxswain – seaman steering ship, or ship's policeman

Cruiser – large warship less battleship

Divisional officer – officer in charge of division

Duck suit – material cotton duck

Kit – clothes issued

Leave – time ashore (holiday)

Nozzer – raw recruit

Piped – signal made by boatswains call-whistle

Quarterdeck – after part of ship

Stern – back part of ship

Watch – period of duty